Jellies

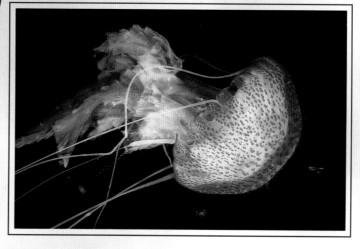

We don't know everything. Even though it seems we must have discovered all the Earth's secrets and named all the stars by now, we haven't. Even very simple creatures like jellyfish hold mysteries that scientists are just beginning to learn about. There are also many jellyfish waiting to be discovered. On page 9 there is a picture taken by Norbert Wu of a jellyfish that scientists have not named yet. Who knows? Maybe *you* will be the scientist who discovers the next new jellyfish!

To my daughters, Rebecca and Caity Pittenger,
who are finding their own way with intelligence and care.

ACKNOWLEDGMENTS
Once again, I thank the remarkable staff of the National
Aquarium in Baltimore for their help and inspiration.

Published by The Millbrook Press, Inc.
2 Old New Milford Road
Brookfield, CT 06804
www.millbrookpress.com

Cover photograph courtesy of © Tim Calver Photography
Photographs courtesy of Animals, Animals: pp. 1 (© Herb Segars), 11
(bottom © O.S.F.), 13 (© Steven David Miller); © Tim Calver
Photography: pp. 2-3, 19, 22-23; © Norbert Wu/
www.norbertwu.com: pp. 5, 6, 8-9, 10 (top), 11 (top), 18, 26, 28-
29; www.norbertwu.com: pp. 10 (bottom © 1995 Peter Parks), 14
(© Ben Cropp), 17 (© Mark Conlin), 21 (© Peter Parks); David
Doubilet/NGS Image Collection: p. 25; George Grall, © National
Aquarium in Baltimore, used by permission: pp. 30-31

Library of Congress Cataloging-in-Publication Data
George, Twig C.
Jellies: The Life of Jellyfish / Twig C. George.— A Millbrook Press
library ed.
p. cm.
Summary: Describes the physical characteristics, habits, and natural
environment of many species of jellyfish, through simple text and
photographs.
ISBN 0-7613-1659-0 (lib. bdg).
1. Jellyfishes—Juvenile literature. [1. Jellyfishes.] I. Title.
QL375.6.G46   2000   593.5'3—dc21   99-048390

Jellies

The Life of Jellyfish

TWIG C. GEORGE

THE MILLBROOK PRESS   BROOKFIELD, CONNECTICUT

If you were a jellyfish you would have two choices—to go up or to go down. That's it. Two. You would not have a brain, so you could not decide what to have for breakfast or where to go for lunch.

A tiny,
hydromedusan
jellyfish

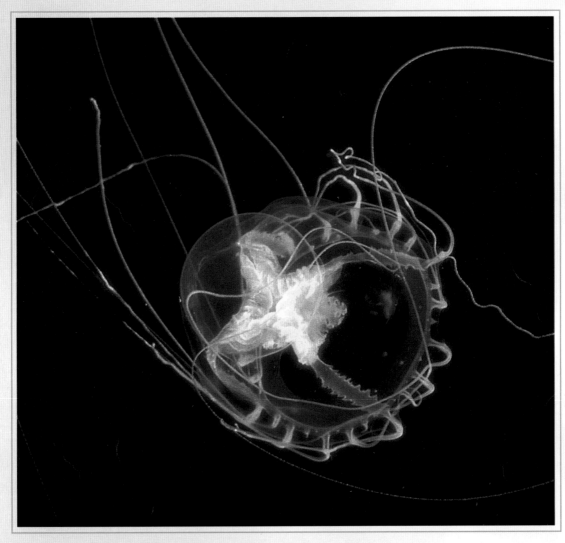

Mangrove jellyfish

The ocean currents would carry you along from place to place. In this way you could travel hundreds of miles. Food might pass by you and get caught in your tentacles. Or not.

Sea turtles, dolphins, and whale sharks would try to eat you.

An unnamed jellyfish

You wouldn't worry about it because you couldn't.

You would just float on.

Rhizostone
jellyfish

Comb
jellyfish

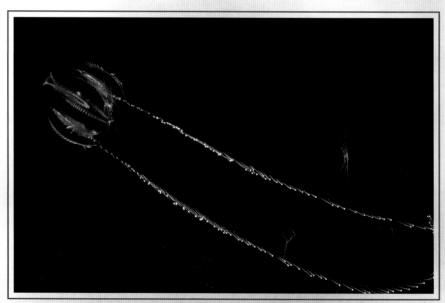

ou would protect yourself with millions of tiny, mechanical cells that, when touched by another animal, release a chemical and sting. Like a bow and arrow. You would not know if you were stinging a friend or an enemy. You would not even know what a friend or an enemy was!

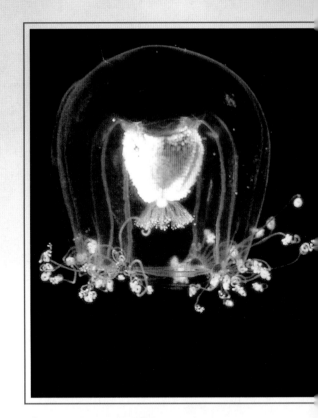

Anthomedusan jellyfish

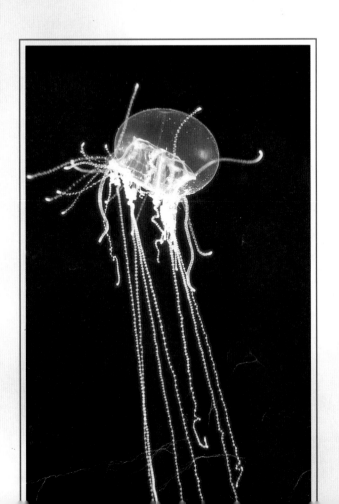

Cigar jellyfish

Jellyfish sting for protection and to catch food. That's all. They don't hunt and they can't chase. They just bump and sting. Bump and sting.

Little fish swim
in and out
of the dome of
this moon jellyfish.

Some jellyfish sting gently. Some jellyfish have a sting so powerful that they are more dangerous than a cobra. These are the Australian box jellies.

Australian box
jellyfish

Jellyfish are so simple that they look like plastic trash floating in the sea. When an animal eats a jellyfish it stays healthy and strong. When an animal eats plastic it gets weaker and weaker and eventually dies.

Thimble jellyfish

Upside-down
jellyfish

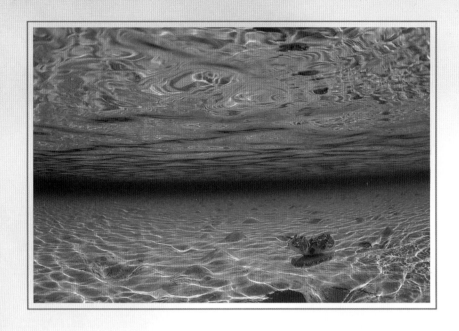

Some jellyfish lie on the shallow bottom in clear, warm seas and grow their own food. These are called upside-down jellyfish. Once they have eaten small bits of algae, just once, they can grow more inside their bodies by sitting in the sun. They are their own greenhouses and grocery stores all wrapped up in one.

To be a jellyfish you need to be shaped like a bell, with at least one mouth, and tentacles. Many animals called jellyfish are really something else. The Portuguese man-of-war is not a real jellyfish. It has an air-filled bubble instead of a water-filled bell.

Portuguese man-of-war

Jellyfish are almost all water and a little protein. They look slimy and disgusting when they wash up on the beach.

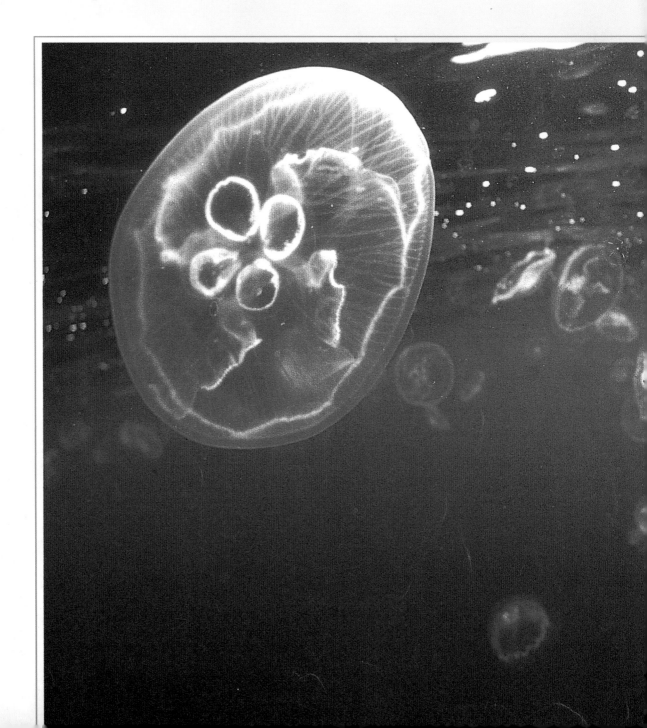

Moon jellyfish

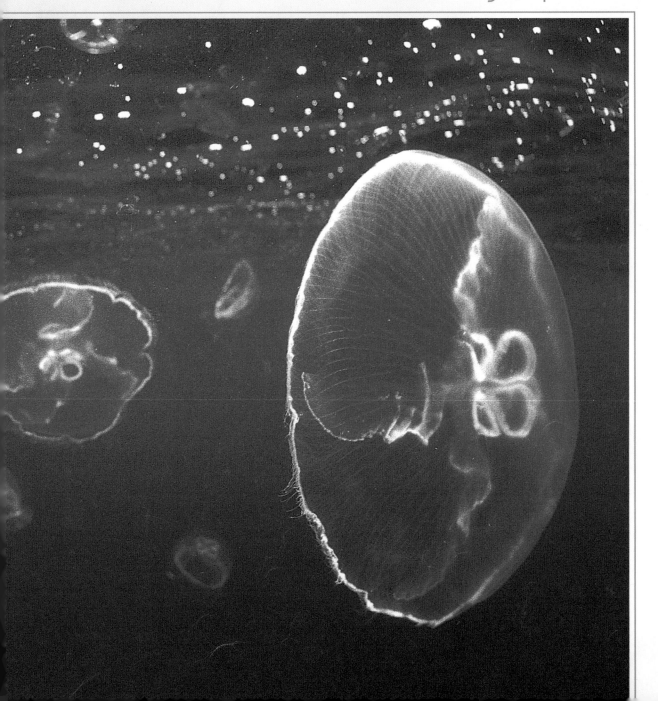

In the sea, jellyfish are beautiful. There are jellyfish as big as basketballs with long red tentacles, called West Coast sea nettles.

West Coast
sea nettle

Oikopieura
labadorensis

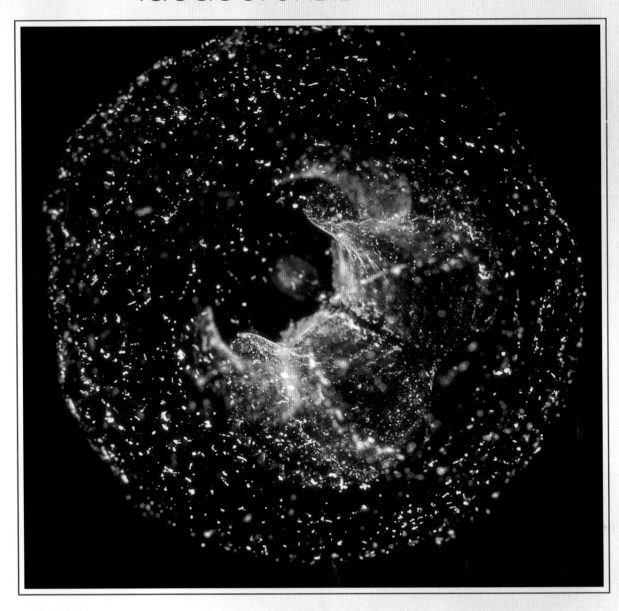

There are tiny, elegant jellyfish that look like a blizzard of snowflakes.

There are jellyfish that grow so big that they are as long as a blue whale. They are called Arctic lion's mane jellyfish. They pulse and drift. They eat and reproduce. They live and die. All without a brain or a heart.

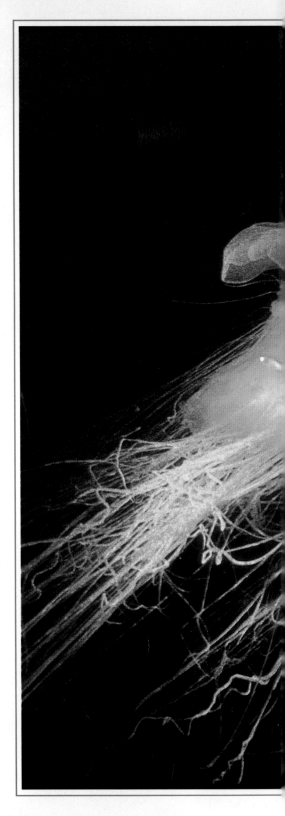

Arctic lion's mane jellyfish

Someday you might be very lucky and see an ocean full of jellyfish. And, since you have a brain and a heart, you would know you were seeing something unforgettable.

Golden
Mastigias
jellyfish

About the author

Twig George grew up surrounded by wildlife. By the time she graduated from high school, her family had raised and released 173 wild animals, not counting their dogs and cats. She often went to sleep with raccoons curled up in her bed, and awoke to crows knocking on the window to come in for breakfast.

These early experiences led to her continued love of the natural world. As an adult, she became interested in conservation education and worked for the Center for Marine Conservation in Washington, D.C. Her husband, David Pittenger, is director of the National Aquarium in Baltimore, Maryland.

The Aquarium has been a major part of Twig's family life. It was the first outing for both her daughters, two days after they were born. Since then the girls have spent thousands of hours entranced by the inhabitants of the natural-like exhibits.

Twig's first two books, A DOLPHIN NAMED BOB and SWIMMING WITH SHARKS, were inspired by the Aquarium's largest and, to some people, most captivating species. With JELLIES, she explores the less-known and less-appreciated animals that nonetheless need our understanding.

Twig, David, Rebecca, and Caity live in Cockeysville, Maryland.